ACCENTS

POEMS 2013–2017

Also by Daniel A. Harris

Poetry

Random Unisons (2013)
Loose Parlance (2008)

Literary Criticism

Tennyson and Personification: The Rhetoric of 'Tithonus' (1986)
Inspirations Unbidden: The 'Terrible Sonnets' of Gerard Manley Hopkins (1982)
Yeats: Coole Park and Ballylee (1974)

This book is composed in Bembo font.
Book design by Sally M. Freedman
Printed and bound by Maple Press

ISBN: 970-0-692-85296-5

ACCENTS

POEMS 2013-2017

Daniel A. Harris

My thanks to the editors of the following magazines, where the following poems in this volume first appeared.

Bryant Literary Review. "Growing Up, Worlds Apart"
California Quarterly. "In a Museum: On Viewing An Oversized Photo"
Chautauqua Literary Journal. "Trench"
Clavier. "Out of Trenton, into the Sourland Mountains, West of Hopewell"
Clark Street Review. "Choosing Performances"
Cold Mountain Review. "On the Rim of the Grand Canyon of the Yellowstone River"
The Connecticut River Review. "When"
CURA: A Literary Magazine of Art and Action. "Coming to Voice"
Ibbetson St. Press. "Down"
Iodine. "For Some Box from Tiffany's"
The Kerf. "During This Heavy Snowfall; Between Moons"
The Listening Eye. "Figuring It Out"
Lullwater Review. "Firefly"
Skidrow Penthouse. "The Dash"
Slant: A Journal of Poetry. "What About Speaking?"
Poem. "Filaments of Fire"

Credits:

Cover image: Islamic tile; pwollinga.www.fotosearch.com

Color Plates follow p.34:
    K. E. McClellan, photograph of John Brown's tombstone, ca. 1896 (courtesy of the Library of Congress, LC-USZ62-107590)
    Intertidal Zone Shoreline, Inside Passage, Alaska (author photograph)

For David,
who crossed the color line

CONTENTS

CHURNING VOICES

Messages

Original Breath (New York City, 1942)

**The Congress of Racial Equality (CORE)
was founded in Chicago.**

Birthed am I, gasping in breaths of white air
      (in that hospital, air for whites only),
colorless, odorless as the presorted airs
      of an iron lung;

I, untainted by breaths of any one
      smit with black lung disease or faces
swabbed with coal-dust; no blackface grease
      for an onstage mime to ape any bodies
      with black skin disease—

and thus: not needing extra scrubbing
      (nor my back a whipping),
because I breathe out no black breaths
      from black black lungs
      that rage for any airs at all

Sleeping Car Porters, Grand Central Station (age 8, 1950)

In *Henderson v. United States*, the Supreme Court ruled that segregated seating in railroad dining cars is unconstitutional.

Not there, in my parents' apartment,
and not in the other grey birds'-nests
built up on Park Avenue,

where no one "kept help" that was black,
but hired only the Irish or German or Polish
as maids for them, cooks for their dinners

(fronds of these Catholics the same on Palm Sunday),
and not among service-men, workmen
they flirted with, kissed (whether tipsy

or not), down in the basement (the cubicles),
and not among doormen (allotted
some few breaths of fresh air), and not

at my day-school, where the nurses on staff,
permitted to touch us, were white
as the janitor (no other kinds mentioned

until seventh grade—but that was only
in textbooks): and so, since not
in those places   where?

(I have won-
dered), and when?
was the first time
I saw one,
woman or man,
a Negro?

The first I saw I did not know at first I saw

behind mahogany doors, step by step down   from the
terminal's bustle,   into the cavernous hollow, the platforms
between the dark tracks those shadowy bodies in shadows
moving: too dark to see the glow of their faces, those invisible
ones underground,   lugging the handcarts with trunks
of the passengers (my own trunk somewhere lost), unseen
by people peering through murks of light   amidst diesel fumes,
in lurch to find their coaches brushing past the conductors
(also not noticed, these too,   more dark ones, though they
the only ones who could direct them to the train-cars, the ones
who worked between the grooves where the journeys began,
the engines inch by inch pulling against the steel rails

these, or their kind, the first   I did not know I saw
until they came among us, into the bright coaches
our pods, visible now as the polished fixtures—

maybe there, on those sleeping cars, Pullmans
(ingenious) that glided us north overnight?—
our clutch of private-school youngsters shipped off
to summer camp, beyond Lake Placid, far
north of the city, so sticky-hot, muggy,
from Grand Central Station prowling forth, then

maybe there, those two porters who made up
our beds, quick-flipped the seats below, and then
with deft invisible twists of the wrist
(astounded, we gazed) unlocked from the sky
of the car those overhead secret berths,
disclosed the envied stowaway places:

magic trickster-men, uniform jackets
spotless white, starched, smoothing with flawless tucks
white sheets for fugitive boys. *Assign me,*
please, to an upper berth, there to drift off,
O, airborne, to lullaby clacks of wheels,
raised high in that secret crib swayed to mirth.

Hands of them I saw then: strange as deep-dyed
velvet gloves, shadowy fingers that shaped
our futures. Visages dark, masks of black
or brown flesh above stiff collars; bright gleams
of teeth dazzling through obedient mouths;
frizzled hair fringing caps. I looked, surprised,

still freed from staring—I, not yet much trained
to see though them (as: "not meant to be seen").
Did I hear them speak? (Were they permitted
speech if not addressed?) Such strangers (and I
their ward, quietly groomed for mastery,
accustomed to being served), guardian guides

spiriting me quick! quick! through Harlem, up
the Hudson, through a rhythmic haze of dreams,
to hear, in the green North Woods, messages
fragrant with balsam, fir, and birch—I, spared
a muffled cry to spy the Big Dipper,
North Star, or spot some hoped-for midnight host

at a safe house, candle in its window,
mindless of underground rails as we passed,
before dawn, through North Elba (where John Brown
homesteaded last, so my mother told me)
to birth me next morning, from my warm shell,
into wilderness. And granting me too:

their message of themselves, figures I touched
with my eyes then, beholding their spectrum
of chocolates, umbers, browns at such close-range
against the overhead lights—too soon withdrawn
as one of them pulled a curtain to close
off my berth—too soon pinched out of my sight,

their kind not to be glimpsed again (not found
among the camp help) until homeward bound.
Their kind of difference: skin-tone, feature.

                                        Mine,
I learned a month later when, though I sang
"Onward, Christian Soldiers!," every Sunday,
with my eager unbroken alto voice

in the white prim church down the rutted road,
an older boy smacked my face with the sting
of this name: "kike." Word till then unheard. *What,
I had to go home to ask, does 'kike' mean?*

                                        Not
often to my hearing hissed.

                    But did they,
alone, bandy it much?—that bite that snaps
                    at skin and bone.

Another Book (age 9, 1951)

At the United Nations, Paul Robeson presented an anti-lynching bill directed at the United States ("We Charge Genocide").

Here, by me: sit on this couch. Last year I gave
    you a book, remember?—a child's book *to begin*
    for you, a child, about Booker T. Washington,
    to tell him   a slave (you made a cute joke,
    "Was he bookish?"), child of slaves without
    the right to read   on "naked earth" raised
    among the quiet floral chintzes of this room
    until by Lincoln freed to read and write books
    (as we do), freed to learn how he might possess
    his name, without dread   *of being bloodied*
        temperate, but also an ember to spark
    his Tuskegee Institute   germinal for his people,
    students, faculty, now freedmen allied side
    by side in works of books and crafts: realizing
    himself freed to be servant to his kind   tinder
    for the slow burn   of new flame

Here, take now   *again among these figurines*
    of pastoral boys and girls in Staffordshire glaze
    this second book, on Harriet Tubman, runaway
    slave from Maryland's Eastern Shore, declared
    the "Moses of her people," leading them freedom-
    wards, by ones or pairs, dragging her footprints
    through forests, downed timber, then back again
    to rescue more. Her head dizzied mad by a chunk
    of metal her master cast: headstrong, running
    her railroad "underground" (off-track but true north):
    intent, long before that great war, to free her kind.

"Is it — ?" No. Not an early birthday gift.
    A book you need now   *it is because of what*
I see you crouch in your carpeted room,

your universal dictionary a free hand's reach away,
free at last of need to sound your syllables: imagine now
blossoms of freedom to write and read at all:
that tingling fragrance of unsnuffled inhalation.

But I hear you think *(as I extend this pearly arm,*
its bracelet of gold whose charms and trinkets
have always intrigued you, heart and locket
and shells) a perturbation tingle in their chimes?—
"What does 'kind' mean?"
                              Let me tell. Of a different
     kind from us   their colors; hair and voices, scent,
noses not shaped like ours: slaves, offsprung from slaves.
For every liberty, petty or great, they needed to claw
(that Washington, politely).
                              Often castaways, endangered
by   our kind. Unknown heroes to   their kind. Wrestling
for what   our kind takes for granted: the standing upright
without grovel, the swing of arms unchained, hugging
whom and when they choose   *how their guts were made*
so twisted by others' denials   (somewhere in the entrails,
belly of my mind, I also made turbid by their lives).

When I was your age   *a little older*
     no one gave me such books   *ignorance:*
     a tree stripped of leaves, winter's skeleton,
     made blind to light   but some I found anyway:
how the Negroes had been vested
     though my parents chose   I should not know
     about this country   their own grandparents coming
     freely (pressured), from Germany to these shores
with voting rights and property, after the Civil War—
then stripped by treacheries   *but still surveilled,*
     whitening differently   from other kinds   of white people,
     learning how to pass   among the Christians.
Young, I was furied (as you too may 'pass through
such a phase')   *though their kind dare not pass*
through such a phase in public.

The porters who came among you in that sleeping car:
your surprise, remember?—dark faces, efficient hands dark.
But also: on that train you were among them part of our history
(so: the air among us always, our currents in swirl)
                                        but you will not
see them   on this Avenue where we live
     nor I at your age   those black or brown
descendants of survivors   of downsouth
        but they cannot be invisible   *you must not go blind*
in fogs of fib   being present among each other

Here, then: this book on Tubman.
Read, come tell me of this woman: Tubman.

Soon you must master harder prose.

From my palm, take: *this precious ingot shaped by flame.*

     O, his fingers it will burn, I see my son's ears   crackle
to frizz, angled knots of cauliflower   he hardly knows that word:
"slave" (outburst like shrapnel): the long stooped rows, fields
of cruelty   from dawn to late dusks   pastoral mire
among the   downsouth nostalgias   among and over us
all: shrouds of abuse   the white sheets splashing flame
He will run   from this room: run now!

Yes, you will need a dictionary for   hard words   *frothing*
to hound you down   consonants fanged
     freechattel, freelabor, freewhip, freerape, freebabyslaves,
     —and yes, being alert, dismayed, you will blurt:
"Who has blacked out those words? Why are they undefined?
Why are the dictionaries made beyond use?"
     (But will he cry out for stopples?)
I cannot utter   do not || not || never || remember(ed) deaths
     of Negroes burnings || of their houses, bodies ||
their several parts disseered: souvenirs of lynchings, riots
against them   happening   how could I know   in my youth
     In this spacious land where I later learned || did not

(who told?) brute acts   against Negroes
        happening of course by happenstance
        St. Louis   Chicago, where the white ones stoned   a Negro boy
for swimming   at the impermissible beach   o! that red summer | |
        such incidents   to happen still | | as you mature   their hap
(and yours): this, the harder prose *that you, a young master,*
        must master: the terrors wrought   by white men, whitewomen
onlooking   (but not me) | | this, your fortune   of lordship
(your happenstance also, you spawn of freeborn immigrants)

Half-truths now I tell him   razor-sharp as clamshells
        The Negroes, denied, are entitled,
        many people think them   *"not"* | | flee them,
            will not let them buy   near them   *contaminant*

conjugate: we lied   have lied   are owned by our lies
        about equality of persons   do not own up

You will plead to know more but   *I am wearied of speech*
if you ask me again, I shall say: *"Burn more incense. To me*
        in your devotions, offer   a fatted calf."

Let the books coax you *(as my bracelet's charms,*
fobs on a keychain) to unlock
these histories   *which I scream but cannot tell aloud*

Oracles dare not burn, my son, the ears of anyone;
        fear to speak without riddle, in candor, aloud;
        some their own tongues swallow, lest their truths be heard
        and they   never again   be neared in dread

Later I shall tell you, *Explode the silences;*
so long as we say nothing, we collaborate;
        learn: you cannot be a bystander

[Back in my room with this new book, its cover flaunting orange,
I turn from my lead soldiers, our Revolutionaries,
against the British troops to secure our liberties, but

What will become of my strongbox   whose key
of brass I polish   key to the hoard, treasures I fondle:
the simulated parchments with their dreamy untruths written
that all men   are created   (were not)   equal
in the Declaration, the Constitution or the Bill of Rights
inalienable only in the Emancipation Proclamation,
   which came loo late)

to read   *and what will be written in my history books?*
about   *that Civil War   who will teach me, how,*
about   *the founders' lies embroidered in their fantasies,*
   stitched as in that room of chintzes?

She said: sift for   right words   in proper places,
   even when they hurt: wrong names
   are untruths   we live among them,   they among us

It was that afternoon I resolved not to mutter any more
the jingle Dicky Mitchell taught me in school—
   Eeenie, meenie, meinie mo,
   Catch a nigger by the toe,
   And if he hollers, let him go—
   eenie, meenie, meinie, mo . . .]

Drumsticks (age 10, 1952)

Ralph Ellison's *Invisible Man* was published.

So here they were   (seen in broad daylight
not underground)   and now striding south
of Harlem's limits   breaching the boundary set,
97th, where the train tracks emerge,   scouting
the gilt of the Avenue   marching in protest

strutting right under the awnings, passing
the uniformed doormen gilded for service,
sedate as the awnings (dark grey or blue),
poised to hail taxis for businessmen leaving
their cloisters of wealth, leaving their wives

who would saunter out later   none of them
needing to study their very own skins (so pale!),
though some of them knew they were wrongwhite
        (Jewish), not Anglowhite,

this phalanx of teens, the three of them wearing
I have forgotten   what   never saw   their blur
from a block away saw them, between me
and my building   knew I couldn't   make it home
but you will not see them   on this Avenue

where (and how) we live   before something
might happen, so I tried to act normal
like a nocolor boy, invisible, not afraid of
Negroes or teens or both, hoping for a tame
or not–encounter, just a nod of the head

if they would only walk stonefaced in unsight,
right past me, boy barely ten, barely tall
enough to cower wherever makeshift cover
might be found, but they kept marching, right there
in the afternoon daylight   right up to my chest,

their eyes pushing my face back, as if they owned,
    droit du seigneur   the Avenue, or me   or were owed
the whole stretch of Avenue, and I owing
now   whatever they asked, and oneofthem
now barkingout from thethreeofthem

Give me those drumsticks
        (that I played at my school on the snare-drum,
        brought home each day for practice)
and didn't shove me, but gave me   *I said,*
                            another chance:
give me your drumsticks, "boy"! and I shaped

a smile to say, *Sure, why not?* (their   *whiplash*
remembered), without protest or whimper, and
surrendered the shellacked sticks, mine,
out of my hands to the Negro teens   just
relieved they didn't beatmeup, bruise and brand

me with strikes, hits from my drumsticks, or stomp
me. But only robbed, because I was younger
and wrongcolor (and they right there on a lark,
my home street, *their street also, further north*),
no one nearby to witness my unrights

and shame. And then, on the very longest of all
the thousand gliding elevator rides
up to the eighth floor, not daring to tell
my mother of that skirmish, how somehow
I lost my drumsticks down there on the street

    (*notmyfault*), there on the far-below street,
as she sometimes made catty slurs about
"the Negroes" that made me blanch, or shudder
that she might say such things again, and wonder
why she'd given me those books on heroes

in revolt (Harriet, skull-smit; that man who taught)—
the small parade that marched through my mind
all the way to free soil, one way or the other,

as if their children's children, some who swaggered
down the Avenue now, had gotten smirched
more blackly when or because
      I didnotunderstandit
they fled north,
and lived among us but not close by
but is   *their kind so different that she acts*
sometimes as if they're beneath
                    dirt, and if

they've been shut apart from their human rights, or ours,
could she please tell me why we still sing
those songs she taught me, *the ones by Stephen Foster*
she loves to play at the piano, with all
their sweet darkies
                "longing for de' old plantation"?

Having Asked My Father about His Ride Back from His Office (age 11, 1953)

In June the Rev. T. J. Jemison, of Baton Rouge, Louisiana, led the first boycott against segregated busing, a tactic adopted by the Rev. Dr. Martin Luther King, Jr., through the will of Rosa Parks.

"Why, yes," replied my father,
"very nice.
             I had a nice
taxi-driver drive me home
from work.
           A Negro, but quite
nice. We had a nice chat.

"I could see part of his face
in the rear-view mirror:
                         nice-
looking, as he raised his eyes,
tilting his head up and rightwards
trying to catch my eyes
                    not sullen,
like some of them"

Studying Latin (age 12, 1954)

**In *Brown v. Topeka, Kansas, Board of Education*,
the Supreme Court ruled unanimously (May 17,
1954) that "in the field of public education, the
doctrine of 'separate but equal' has no place.
Separate educational facilities are inherently
unequal. Therefore, we hold that the plaintiffs
and others similarly situated for whom the
actions have been brought are, by reason of
the segregation complained of, deprived of the
equal protection of the laws guaranteed by the
Fourteenth Amendment."**

In that rare Manhattan school accepting sons
of Jews, free offspring of safe immigrants (some
just barely escaped from Hitler)—Horman,
Perlman, Rosen, Wechsler, Sackler, Stein (names
    mine once resembled),

I first confronted Latin: elegant tongue
of the Republic; next, the bloodied language
of empire: secular, sacred, chiseled signage
of demands. For us that Latin was barely fledged,
    no enemies yet to subjugate.

Mr. Gamble, our master: his suit ever-grey
(no commoner's tunic, this citizen's toga), breast pocket
handkerchief blooming; polished, his shoes, mirror-gleam black.
He wore the discipline he taught. Badged navy-
    blue blazers, ours.

Each day: vocabulary before grammar,
the nouns before verbs, the ranking of persons
as "subjects," shortly demoted to foreign
"objects" by a suffix (curt): the actor's
    voice-box gored, only ears left—thing acted on.

Then: the grids for time, verbs and their agents:
the past neatly packaged, futures tenses
parceled starkly as prophesies thundered,
hooted by voices hidden: Aeolian breezes
thrumming laws of diction; chokeholds
    held against windpipe until well-schooled—

(Mister Glenn Gamble   training young masters
    slaves to his homework   students in study)

Today (*hodie*): this item, a puzzle
to the child at his homework last night:
    "*servus, - a,*   noun = servant, slave"
      ("from *servare*, v.t. [verb transitive] = hold, keep")

—Why the two definitions? Yes, his mother kept "help"
(the cook, a maid to wait on table, dust, make beds)—
    but not her slaves?

So: what about those other *serviae* [fem.]?
    Therefore, to ask: "Sir, why does just one word
      mean so differently?"
    "Because the word embodies a legal category of persons
unfree, yet bound to their masters under two different
circumstances while expressing the same bondage to labor
(service or servitude), the financial contract (so to speak)
at variance in each instance."

Oh. Yoking of mule and donkey; zebra. How
to untangle such knots of slippery hands
(suave, but not like those porters')
that wove the little world he knew,
and discover who, by such stitching,
might gain by such knotting?—

the same slips of tongue he'd found
in his slight Hebrew: the *eved,*
"servant, slave," also confounding
rank and economic status:

We were slaves in the land of Egypt (he read at Passover),
    surely not "servants" harvesting those great yields of brick.
And Hagar?—handmaid or slave for Abraham's use?

Why did people not use proper words
in proper places? Thus, persisting after class:
    "Sir, did the Romans 'hold' or 'keep' slaves?"
"Why, yes. From all over, so Caesar tells us: *omnia Gallia*,
beyond the Pontus, throughout the Mediterranean seas, Africa,
a rainbow from foreign shores, to work the *latifundia* solely
for the owner's profit. Another new word. Rather like the
plantations down South.
    But now: our lesson in grammar. History must wait."

Tremble in the walls, this floor now a chasm
releasing to surface the many-winged beasts
of the night snorting flame, flying towards noon.

There, too, in ancient Rome, more than a few.
Omnii servii, so many worldwide?—not only
downsouth, not just Tubman and Washington:
more than the crop just spiking up with the boles
in American History; amidst the Spanish moss, wisteria.

Plantation-owners, owning plantations?   —Yes;
also owned slaves as servants subjected?   —Yes;
no: objected. As free labor?   —Yes.

Work to break backs?—Yes. He flinched at   *freewhip*
lashes in his mother's mind, and swallowed
stench of nausea distasting his glottis;
gristle of dooms, machines of abuse
and tumult dismantled by a war?

And free cotton: white men
the buyers of black things or persons,
bought from other white men
who got, fetched them somehow?   —Yes.

(or else the slaves   had always been
there naturally   blooming with the boles
a fresh crop each year, or newly transported
since the harvested bales were sent somewhere)
From where transported?— I suggest you ask the new American
    History teacher, Mr. O'Connell.
From distant shores, the Atlantic like the Mediterranean?—
                                       Ask Mr. O'Connell.
And how transported? *or welcomed?*   Ask him.

Here, just three blocks from home at 81st,
he dangled between ancient, present
powers of the Western world he knew
so little about—both, slave-holding,
slave-consuming to gain more gain—
a mesh of shadows knotting him tight.

Fluffs of the blooms in his brain-cage rattling;
like pebbles, without rest buffeting.

Servare again: to "hold" or "keep"—
if slaves for their masters worked, why,
despite Mr. Gamble's definition, could they not
also be servants? paid like Josephine, their servant
maid, dressed as his mother chose (in black,
her apron white). But maybe paid a pittance,
plus room and board? Unfree labor: his first black dawn.

More: when a master commanded his *servum* (object),
how might a guest discern if he addressed a what
or a whom—the same (object) having the same body—
or not? Would the bystander's view of the master change
(as if he were to note his father now wore a new Paisley tie)
if he learned the master kept a slave, and not simply
a servant? Could you see the difference without asking—
or were taught to note by color of skin? (Never had he seen
dark ones serve in apartments of his friends' parents).
Did something change in the syllables *servus* (n.) that he could
not read or pronounce? Was the noun alive? did something

inside make it bulge (seedling, infant whelk), shape-changing
creature that could snap the servant (*servus*) into a thing
(*servus*, slave)? *Fire of magma for stones to be kicked—*
more haunting than fire of dragons, rake of their claws.
  Or was it the prefix attached to the noun
that propagated new verbs?—en-slave—and thus
the new persons (slav-er, en-slav-er) who did
the enslaving, making humans things. Suffixes also.

Mister Glenn Gamble   training young masters   attentive
  to the swerves   of prefix and suffix   slaves
  to his homework   but never lashed for learning

Grappling hooks, such chain-links of language,
of more allure than the oracle's bracelet of trinkets

Thus the en-slav-er: of nouns, the seedlings.
"No things are so by nature but verbs do make
them so." *Servare* = to hold, keep. The noun-
in-transit by a command-er command-ed
to be an ob-ject. *The verb?—a simple term*
of power, not nature, the exertion of control
by one body over another. As she had said:
Use proper words. (In verbs begin responsibilities:
for the thing, products of its body owned
by those who sought some finer arts, or company
of friends, lacking skill to clear their fields
for cotton, grapple with their crops (and maybe
to grasp without scruple the courtly life
of subsidy from things so near to hand,
in custody—responsibilities disowned).

Mister Glenn Gamble   had noted of Horace: 'a slave;
  you will read him later; manumitted by his master'
  (another new word).

How then to parse that what or whom that's made
of words? Slave, then freed slave, then the freedman who served

his kind, but never "fugitive" like Harriet (each category of noun
to master, as if a tense, always draped in the nearly naked skin
of his first names ("slave" and "nigger," "darkie," "Negro,")?—
never named a man   free by birth, unbroken
        degrees of persons   rights to personhood   smudged

handed over for a sum by persons,
shadowy enslavers (the plantation-owners only
end-users of slaves, spared the en-slaving,
just using the commerce. The owners "had" slaves,
or so he'd read in history books he'd read in youth,
but now he didn't know what "having" meant
or where and how the getting happened.
Did the enslavers just pack them up   *on foreign shores*
        and ship them overseas?

How to unearth the secrets? some slaves
he'd read about   but didn't know any Negroes
now who could tell him (except the ones
who could have   beatenhimup
        for the sake of his drumsticks,
        for the sake of some strange fruit
        swallowed, proffered by their parents?)
They wouldn't come to him, so how would he
        search for them   ask them with a tremulous decency?—
here, where he lived in the upnorth almost
segregated among   his kind, learning
of slaves from Latin and books,   and his mother,
who had handed him, just this June,
a copy of *The New York Times,*
pointing to the banner headline reading,
"High Court Bans School Segregation,"
and urging: "Here, you need to read
this article—our Supreme Court has ruled
that segregated schools are unconstitutional.
Brown versus Topeka Board of Education."
        He was sure he believed in integration
but didn't know anyone in his school

who was integrated.   What could "separate
but equal" mean if he couldn't talk
to anyone who was "separate"?

At the Boundary (age 13, 1955)

**In Mississippi, Emmett Till was lynched (August).
In Montgomery, Alabama, a white bus-driver
deliberately moved the "Colored" sign in his bus
further back, so that he could order Rosa Parks
to give up her seat (December).**

Not steam but wind-rush of bulk, engine's glare-light
from rails underground speed to the viaduct,
slice over cars to tracks that vault above: a blur

echoing rattles of wheels gone: mute cutout
where that train just was. Turn north: squint, catch
that speck. Pigeons flock back to bob and peck.

Here is where it happens: here all the trains explode
to day. Spiked palings ring the mouth of this tunnel.
Press over; hoot   *recall the porters, conductors*
                  What inhabits that channel

whose unmeasured tracks are the spine of life buried
beneath Park Avenue?—forget-met-nots above,
in season white lilies, clipped-grass islands shadowed

by blocks of apartments, shields of limestone stacked,
kept plush. Gilt and tacit brags of class: sidewalks
swept; traffic lanes free of buses, noises

of commerce. But north?—those people unknown,
squat brownstones painted with ads; billboards,
laundry flapping in the wind. ("Do not," *warned*

my father) "do not stray past 96th; recall
those Negro   boys: your drumsticks, they stole." At just
this one block more, at 97th, my post: to resist

Manhattan's color line, where whiteland shades
to off-limits Harlem (where they have not trod . . .
those tongues so strange, their garb): here, on this edge,

this same season that Marian Anderson
breaks the color line at the Metropolitan,—
in the cross-hairs to stand here now, thirteen, pubescent

at this point of south and north, above below:
to peer through scrims, diaphanous shrouds hung,
thrall to rumbles deferred, the next explosions
                    from down there, and the dreams.

Visiting John Brown's Farm (age 15, 1957), North Elba, in the Adirondacks

In September, Orval Faubus physically blocked the entry to the Little Rock Central High School to prevent school integration. The Southern Christian Leadership Conference (SCLC) was founded, with the Reverend Dr. Martin Luther King, Jr., as chair (January).

I. The Homestead

Here, on this knoll in these High Peaks, mountains
whose igneous bedrock is kin to stone of the moon,

here, where he birthed the phases of his raid, where they buried
his body after the botch at Harper's Ferry—

all is as she said while driving me here:
    "He was an Abolitionist before Garrison
             (I tell you new names again).
When he was your age, perhaps older, he saw a white man

beat 'before his eyes with Iron Shovels or any other thing
that came close to hand' a Negro boy, and vowed then

to defy all his life the law of the land" (*I don't know how
I learned that truth*). I see acres of history cruelly sown

among us (Tubman again searing my mind, that stone
                    striking her head):
this place where that arsenal is assembled, all scumbled,
              the blood

everywhere soaking through Indian paint-brush,

that orange flower burnt with his wrath blazoned.
Being here stuns me, proves what I'd heard: the craze

of the downsouth planters to shackle   *objects freelabor*   their slaves
to the white prickled cotton-fields spiked like nettles.

Who'd contrive

such insurrection (risking his last sons', dear sons' blood)
without the more than just, sufficient cause to tread

that bondage under? Her pilgrimage now: "to stand here,
where he became crystal: soaking up, flashing fire."

Our feet to tread the places   *where the grapes*
of wrath are trod   "child (still), such barest traces,

those books I gave you—then, my only medium."
Could she, loath to scar, have spoken more? "Now come,

to ground he hallowed by the wars of all his decades. Follow him
(seated, coffin-bound, in that bare cart bound to greet his gallows).

He know the precise incendiary weight of his own
white death to his cause,
and certain that no protests of the pen could ever break the curse."
We must "sniff in this air the ripples of his pulse.

You remember, yes?—not from us hidden, not far off
in the heavens or beyond the sea, but on this turf:

North Elba, now." To stand witness to vibrations that station us,
our feet, not far south of Canada, its sanctuaries

(and Ausable Forks, two days' off by the North Star's light,
the underground railroad, another safe house for Harriet's

people, salved). From Lake Placid, where we stay up here, not far.
Enter now his simple clapboard house. Follow. Yes: a farmer's

common things—washstand, bowl; a rocker, plain-style;
narrow double bed, homespun fabrics bare enough to let him mull

in peace his design for justice: arm the Negro bands, help them begin
their own war to free all slaves, the down-trod,

> mastered but unruined.

On a wall, a painting, copied: Brown in his passion,

> his beard a fleece

of lambswool. (His death, cried Emerson, "will make

> the gallows
> glorious like the Cross")—

arms reaching straight from his sides (as Moses' arms lifted, steadied,
to claim triumph from tempest, Kansas now bloodied,

but brandishing Bible and rifle, the gorge of his mouth black
yet unsilenced, crying for the war to break slavery's back.

On a wall nearby, a crinkled typescript of a document from his trial
(October, 1859): his speech after conviction, his covenant with all
the slaves, plain-spoken:

*"I believe that to have interfered as I have done as I have always freely
admitted have done in behalf of His despised poor, was not wrong,
but right. Now, if it is deemed necessary that I should forfeit my life for the
furtherance of the ends of justice, and mingle my blood further with the blood
of my children and with the blood of millions in this slave country whose
rights are disregarded by wicked, cruel, and unjust enactments, I submit;
so let it be done!"*

Reading again: "This slave *country*," not just the South.
And again: "unjust enactments": by lawmakers northern

> as well as from the South—

this white man speaking proper words, his voice piercing
my face, my ears (and I too muzzled still to ask what
my history books would not release), his words

> confirmed by—what?—

the forfeit of his body's life, this white man's indictment,
this crisp howl for justice to my ears, on my lips clamant.

Now at my side my mother comes quietly to explain:

"Brown for years disciplined his body to stand witness
against chattel slavery (legal, yes, but criminal), chose

to offer not less than his complete life (though no burnt holocaust):
his retort to those who bought people, used them for free, wrested

asunder whole families." And adds: "Brown knew Tubman—
In Canada she recruited escaped slaves for him. His name
for her? 'My General.'
                    Your great-great-grandfather Einhorn

(David, his name) also knew Brown. An Abolitionist and rabbi,
he preached and wrote in Baltimore, not far from Harper's Ferry."

—*My who?* —Who? Why haven't you told me before?
                    Please: tell now.
"I saw no need; but our times have changed.
                    Perhaps you'll remain inside a while ... ?"

Did he also know Tubman? (*unknowing, she spreads empty palms*)

"... then come outside" (*remember, she says: to feel under foot
                              this soil again*),
"we'll meet at the pond and to talk as we stroll around."

From a rabbi, my descent from an Abolitionist?
I'm rioted with questions. But Brown's outrage smacks me first:
                    his white witness to justice,

his own red blood shed: not the Negroes in revolt, but one of us,
heir to my color's lordship, refusing white dominion
                              (his, supposed).

Millstones of that ancient war still grind them down.
                    By taxi or car, I've seen
the ragged slums, heard about the South Bronx,
                    stood at the color line.

Two years back, my mother broke to me the tell-tale doom
of Emmett Till. His body mashed in a swamp. His face:
                                                    unwordable.

And now this ancestor Einhorn, rabbi and witness—
do his acts call me to witness also? Is there exit from witness?

II. Outside

Dwarfing a picket fence, his boulder: monumental, huge
as his deeds, "JOHN BROWN, 1859," more starkly gouged

than his headstone, feet away, ringed by asters
unwithered still, this early fall. Its mass blocks my eyes. Haste,
these trenched incisions speak like little knobs of Braille:
                                                    haste to care.
I caress rough granite, scratch my palm, break skin:
                                        what will I dare dare?

Thus he felt cuts on the Negroes' backs as his own,
from the time he saw   *freewhiplash*   those "Shovels of Iron"
(his own hide spared) "or any other thing to hand,"

speech of this boulder's backside facing the pathway (but not
revealed, its hidden visage frontwards: his devotion's burn, secret:

the always tears of his lamentations among rains,
wringing his pitch of penitence for crimes by others done),

this rock of Brown bleeding slow tears to ask
(as I bleed my pittance):
        What did your mother tell
        you about the death of Emmett Till?

Amidst the bracken his face made mush.
His dead scream on my palm an indent of pressure.
Did she tell you about his right eye gouged out,
        his right ear shot off?   —Yes, sir.

John Brown's Graveyard with boulder, ca. 1896, near Lake Placid, NY. (See "Messages," pp. 32-41.)

Intertidal Zone with Starfish, Inside Passage, Alaska. (See "Between Moons," pp. 53-54.)

His human body, thorned by barbed wire, attached
*   to a cotton-gin fan to weight him down?*   —Yes, sir.
Did she speak of the cleaver struck
*   down the middle of his skull?*   —No, sir.
(Some things a mother must withhold: the stunned skulls.)

And what—between his ruin, my hanging—what outrages more
*   have scarred*
still these States in this century you inherit? Are Negroes still unspared,

daily slain, those descendants of survivors, their own children
scythed as these fields in fall? The innocents burnt or lynched?

With my little blood I touch the fissures but cannot respond.
(On days unlike this, you can feel on his face his weeps of rain.)
                                        Today you must imagine.

Have you read the note I gave to a guard at my gallows?   —No, sir.
"I, John Brown, am now quite certain that the crimes of this guilty land
can never be purged away but with blood."   —No, sir.

I did not ask that more blood should be shed after that great purge. But
the aftermath of hate has come, hail in all seasons. I grieve the shed
of blood to come, by pint and gallon.

In a scoop of rockface, I finger his signs:
Bloody red dots: make me a map with red bloody dots to show
*   where the blood*
of blacks has been shed, where whites have terrorized Negro neighborhoods.
This work, to justify his blood   I will need to learn.

Tell me, too, how new southern men have deviously devised new forms
for new slave labor—true as the crow flies, in all but name?

Killings in the cities   he knows I will find, not only
                              on backroads   *in woods;*
and hereupnorth   in broad daylight. Who among Negroes
                              is not still afraid?

Tell where, how often have the rights of Negroes to vote
been X'd out? Follow the scent of Till decayed, rot

in the lies of whites (the original lie of the land), not the dark perfume
of skunk, but from the nation's belly the stench of bad meat consumed.

Try walking through the rock of me if you choose to bypass
                                        this work for justice;
shiver through your summers to think of the blood of my sacrifice.

Those wild wrongs done: abolish them again.
Yes, *find your patriarch, let that Einhorn blood*
                                mantle though my veins.

That white Carian marble body of justice?—daub it jet
black (for once!). Steady the scales others have rigged (*weight*

them towards equity.   Cut through the binding straps
of my swaddling household that have bound me
                                to see the shapes
of Negroes only, in a taxi's rear-window eclipsed.

They are not blocks of obsidian: they will bounce back your stare,
mirror and shatter your face   *if you try walking through them.*
                                        Repair.
"You are not required" (I am taught) "to complete
                                the work of repair;
but neither are you free to desist." If not now, say when.

Your fingers tremble on my lichens.   And if not then
you will sink in a bog. Show me, in the prisons
and ghettoes of despair, how my truth   goes marching on.
        I ask your service.   Asks me, for justice.
These tongues of flame sear my hand.
        In the midst of this clear-cut land,
        furrowed by turbulence, that stone
        marks out new fields to seed afresh,
        marks now the signatures of men

who marked the first sin
of this nation.   This mountain
of Brown, who sat bound in his coffin
    driven to his gallows.

III. At The Pond

"You must have paused," she asks," at Brown's boulder?"
Yes: we conversed; I touched his surface. Mused.
That stone's become "the navel of these Peaks,"
she offers, "and its double, this clear Adirondack pond—
together a simple emblem that asks us
to cast pebbles, make ripples." Again she laments
Till's death ("a boy, your age"), his body wrecked
and cast into the muddy Tallahatchie—"not like
the laps of crystal whitecaps here."
        But there's another reason (her voice stiffens)
she's brought me here now. "Soon your fall term
will begin. Last week, in Little Rock, Arkansas,
the state governor with his own body blocked
the main entry to the Central High School,
and stood there, yes, to block with his body
the entry of any Negro students yet again
made equal by our Federal law. Orval Faubus,
defiant segregationist, fanatic man—in his craw
the spiteful bones of centuries stuck." Never
have I heard my mother speak such wrath before.

I stare at the pond, innocent of battle;
pick up a pebble and chuck; it plops,
not far out—not yet the splash I am asked
to make. I kick turf. My own school-life:

        just as segregated as that school
in Little Rock, I say to her, not I among them,
nor they among us.
                    She frowns at the echo:
"Your father and I" (those edgy parental tones)

would not knowingly send you to any school
deliberately segregated, and of course
they want me to have "the best education." Yes.
                    She bristles more;
I've rubbed against the grain. "Rosa Parks,
fearless—," and turns to face me fully,
"that article I showed you, from 1955 also:
"your world now. Fearless," she quickens,
"impatient with the long waiting of   her kind,
too long bound down: in Montgomery,
Alabama, determined to keep her seat
in a bus, unwilling more to budge for any
white person. *That's when they began to boycott*
the busses." They chose to walk, trudge to work, long miles,
then gave each other rides."
                    Languidly now
we tread this path, skirt this shore around
these waters silky dark in sunshine.

For your generation, "ferment shall come soon,"
fires shall scorch the streets   "Now you will learn
of the White Citizens' Councils, how they work
the hate of the KKK"   (*so little I know*
of those earlier fires, crackling to entertain
the crowds   again   like whiplash)   "and riots."

Yes. But what about the rabbi, from whom
we are descended? My great-great-

— "the rabbi, Einhorn?"—

                    why did you wait to tell me
at John Brown's home, but not before? What
is the sudden need now?
                    "Distinguished
in his time; now forgotten; he stood witness
against the enslaving of Negroes
by slavers and planters: Abolitionist
(as you too will be asked to stand

against injustice: so much for the need).”
      But she has her own questions
(*her own mother, she says, his grand-daughter,*
hardly mentioned him; she knows his name
but has no image)—prophetic like Brown
(“Amalekites” to him, enemies to Jews),
notorious for denouncing a pro-slavery rabbi
in New York—
      She's read so little (all his sermons in German);
      perhaps someday I …?—
within days after gunboats of the Union
fired first shots on Fort Sumter, they all came
to tar-and-feather him, burned down his house
in Baltimore—mobs paid off with planters’ money.
He fled, invited to Philadelphia.
      Search out his writings; soak them in
with this sunlight. “Remember: you carry his bloodline.”
      Yes. *So: the books she gave me years ago.*

We stare into the pond’s riddle
that speaks no riddle: *heft a weightier stone to sink in me*
(open Brown’s black gorge to cry out again).

But you’ve also brought me to this farm, boulder and house,
this pond because I am   (*Brown has asked my service*),
I am to   what does it mean, *I ask aloud,* ‘to stand witness’?
Speak. The voices here are judgments against us.
                                        Yes
(her body slumps a bit, eyes avert. Am I too young
to face a face so shadowed by remorse?)   *she has not*
acted enough (“we never know enough to act in time”),
“though I have sometimes known enough to act and”
was not always only   a Park Avenue wife.

“Don’t be deaf to his gallows-cry.”
My inheritance: the skin of my new name, its inside rough.

“Oppose injustice.” What we’ve read indoors—

she recalls his words about "cruel, and unjust
enactments"—*still they lock this land in chokeholds;*
learn to observe; then dare more than I.
Always name aloud the name of the human agent;
never say of the victim, "brutally whipped"; but name
the man who brutally acts.
     A formula? but candid, I know;
she's troubled to speak what skips her tongue.
     (And again: the suffix of the slav-er,
     own-er, as if she'd studied with old Mr. Gamble
     but speaking out these truths of tongue,
     as if reading from some unknown primer
     at the back of her mind.

"The stripping of Negroes of their rights:
do not accept."
          The sun's at her back, her face
darkened. "It's not right, the way we live
in ignorance: they are part of us, we are part
of them—belong to what we have done, still do
to them," and nags me: *meet them as persons,*
walk out of our apartment cages—

     I shake my head: she hasn't understood
     what I've just asked   about the all-white school
     I walk to every day—
               otherwise
you'll never learn how they are still kicked: stone
things who suffer weathering, as glaciers once scored
Brown's boulder.

"You cannot bystand."
          Which is what? "—What?"
"Bystanding"—she flusters, begins again:
"a bystander—someone who overlooks
suffering or inflicted pain or atrocity

and does nothing. The opposite of
standing witness. Someone who ignores
responsibilities for other people's lives
and rights. Almost a collaborator."

But some context?
"So, since you've never taken me to see Harlem,
have you allowed me to bystand? Not see them,
descendants of survivors? We go to the movies
midtown; why not go further north, uptown?"

She shakes her head: *it would not be safe for us.* "In 1943,
the year after you were born, there were riots there."
What might happen, we don't know. But yes, she nods,
uneasily. "You know, when we drive here, to Placid,
escaping the city's heat—you remember the Negro
children we see playing on the streets in the water
of hydrants opened for them because they have
no place else to go, don't you?"—Yes.—

"I know a thing," she says, *some halfway kinship
with them because of what   all our kind have done
against them.* Not a fetched connection, maybe. "Still
they are shot or burnt, by us stomped down though these
centuries."

She tells me a secret she's loath to say
aloud (*but you are old enough now*): "how
we are still kept out   *they bar us as Jews*
from the country club across the lake at Placid.
That is a little thing these days, though once
it used to sting"—and I am stung now:
Here in the mountains? against us, there is prejudice?
"Oh yes, my dear,"   *of course they've tried to hide it
from me*—"oh yes, my dear!" (*your father's found
another golf courses where he can play*)—
"—a nothing weighed

against the nothings we have all made
of Negroes' lives, even though we're Jews
and, she says, "you attend a school
whose head master tolerates   our kind."

And we dare not measure, she says, the damage done
to them   as damage less   than done to ours,
or dismiss what's theirs   as bystanders.
        (And never forget: we came to these shores free,
        not in chains and naked.)

"Let me shape for you a puzzle:
their skins, their features are
their yellow star.

"Soon you will learn of Europe and beyond, the kings
        and mobs who for a thousand years   robbed us,
        kept us in ghettoes   exiled and banished us
        (*and you will read: burned and murdered us*)

the untold many   *the many untold   not told yet*
(*it is only 1957; no one yet speaks much of what was done*)

But we were never bought, enslaved as naked chattel, not even
when we were transported   *put on forced-marches*   to Babylon

This is why I feel affinity.

Someday soon he will learn more. "Enjoy now
the aromas of cut grass here, sweetly pungent."
        Yes, he wants to query

I want to ask   *perhaps next year when he is older*
"Soon," I hear, "I shall give you another book"—
But why not now?—
        "this one, by Franz Werfel, a true novel,
        about what happened in Armenia, mass murders,
        (we barely have another word yet   *but you will learn it*)

my message for you   in a kind of code
like this visit   to John Brown, his boulder—
In time you will learn   *how to shift*
from those mass killings to this later   is that the word, "genocide"?
which we do not   (too terrible to tell about;
I lost sleep—much)   *yet name   out loud   as a squirrel*
shifts weight   and jumps from limb to limb
though we are not so agile.

. . . .

A boy will someday sit atop that stone
to lend it scale, climb peaks nearby;
yet still not know enough to ask
a thing of Brown, to Brown's
long rage be deaf.

Susurrus of breeze on the pond
chiffon of cloud, some High Peaks mirrored:
rippling grasses and forest under feet reflected
and now, soon to come,
the chills and then the frosts
that shall each night crust fresh snows with ice
to lend sheen of the moon on the stone of him,
barely halfway concealed by ten feet of snow

At the 125th St. Train Station, Harlem
(age 18, 1960, waiting to return to college)

The Student Non-Violent Coordinating Committee (SNCC) was founded that summer and the first sit-ins were organized (Greensboro, North Carolina).

I. Before

—*From Harlem? But dear, why take the train from there?*
—Your mother thinks *it's unsafe to take the train from there.*
—*You can   you can never tell what*
—*Your father says,* leave from Grand Central:
            more   people, more *bright*

II. The Station

Here, after the openwork iron steps,
the long flight up in my foray to cross
the color line they have drawn to keep me
            in their   ownwhite   ghetto

I suppose myself   buffoon or hero
integrating this station elevated
above the street (now in the Waiting Room,
waiting: will I be the only person white?)

Coming early to this maze or cave to see
what they've warned me not to enter —

       some monster at the center of the tangle

—I find a simple room, almost square, and ringed
by slatted benches, its middle a simple blank,
tranquil, tan linoleum scuffed.

A glance around: so few others yet,
barely enough for me to discover myself
segregated, as they have been, removed
not among   from a flock
>   (Latin again: the *grex* = flock or crowd
>   to *se-greg-ate* = *to remove from the flock;*
>   so the prefix *se-* : apart (e.g., *se*-cede = [to] separate
>   from the Union)

They're just randomly spaced, all of them older.
A man slouched, legs splayed; another hunched
over a tabloid; another, suited; and an elderly pair,
quietly staid; the others, women. All, at ease
more than I, jittered in fear they clothe me
in white skin, will seek revenge for damages wreaked.
>   No need to fear the quiet pecking flock
>   that's here. This crowd's not poised to mob me;
>   This room's public; the lights are bright;
>   I won't be hurt tonight.
>   Still, alone
>   this first time   *among them*
>   surrounded   but not wanting
>   to be absent but *meet them as persons*
>   witness   them

III. The Sale

Through the iron black grill: "*I want
a ticket, please. To New Haven.*"—
shy, a bit, to buy a thing from a person
whose kind were bought, broken
up, sold by my kind.

In silence the ticket-master pushes
the ticket under the grill. Why should he pass
me any thing, even change I'm rightly owed?—
he's obliged; it's the man's paid work.
But still he's owed.

The ticket's other cost? my surprise. Did I expect
to be denied the right to buy? refused respect
because of my color, or barred from some school
like Little Rock High. Or he, denied the right to sell?

His shadowed hand, the rash on mine.

IV. Finding My Seat

Off-balanced now: not knowing where to sit
anywhere, where's my right anywhere place to sit—
not from anyone too few or many feet away. Sit?

Am I missing a birthright, some signage
that says What You Are Permitted? On this stage,
of linoleum, my feet burn. All see me fumble to find
        some space acceptable   among the many
empty spaces. I learn and muse   a little irony:
        before Rosa, people knew their place
        (if colored and straying, you could
        be cuffed or clubbed: a native suspect
        without rights, at best a "loiterer")

V. Whose Names

are anonymous. "Offspring of Harriet"?—huddles
of families before them broken, or someone else
whom John Brown's life died to salvage?—
if not still "boy," then what? Still the ghosted haze
        of "slave," that smiting   *whiplash*
type I still do not get past
        as if their fault   somehow not mine
        and I not exempt by recalling the name
of my ancestor rabbi, my shield
        against blame (though I too have no image
of flesh to put on the bone of his name)
        their only name like a placard hung

· 44 ·

around their necks   ("freed slave")
       as if in a spot-lit line-up,
not like—like? the porters with their flashy magic,
molded by their uniform, dressed in names by others given—
who maybe were offsprung from sharecroppers,
just after Lincoln, tilling someone else's fields. (Brown
         has enjoined: explore the recent kinds
         of en-slavement, that dark growth
         inside the noun, unanswered yet.
But these here have slipped their shackles,
their backs no longer bent but risen.)

Shudder through my shame, naming such people
just waiting, like me, to get on a train to go
somewhere they want to go, to visit
a child (not sold downsouth), get back
to a living room, not forced to pick cotton
forcewhipped   or just *forced*
       (all of us sharing the kinship
       of waiting. I so awkwardly).

I have no adjectives, would blurt some wrong ones.
Am prickled they might call me "honky," jibe me
 as "Massa," drape me in the skin of overlordship
I inherit; but how can I tint myself otherwise?—
flesh not being whiteface or paint.
       Finding the right names, truest taint.
       Names: the mallets hammered down at auction.
How to say hello?—to Jimmy, Paul, Harriet.

V. Whose Eyes

I hesitate to meet because of   *what we have done,*
still do. I sneak my glances, as rarely with   my kind.
Is this how they are now, the latter survivors?—
not in rags, now wearing usable shoes, treading forth
to my eyes from the white books, though seated.
       Under bare bulbs, the room pulses;

everyone vibrates against my eyes, protuberant;
into seat or wall, no one blends, but not
        as I don't blend.
More browns than those in my Crayola set
years ago. I study the mottles on my hands, imagine
        these various whites, think of   our own shades:
pale and swarthy, sallow, tanned; the women
who powder their noses, rouge their cheeks. But do
the color-ranges somewhere meet? Their tongues
more pink than ours; the whites of their teeth
more white against their lips, more pearly,
distinct as Monet's poplars at the show
last year. Portraits unframed but not flattened
to silhouettes (already black)
        but can their inside mirrors evade tarnish,
        the defacements of Emmett's face?
And so we sit together along the sides of this room
as in a casual circle joined. I steal
my covert glances, afraid of being noticed.

(I came to view some pictures of the pleased
or worried, sad or bored, the lines of age,
find some commonness with them   but find
that I inherit still the eye of some   master
who jerks a jaw to inspect before buying
off the block—decades past, no kin of mine.
        The cartilage in my left ear aches; my staring hurts.
        My parents taught me: keep your eyes to yourself—
            though they've stared through so many.
        Break your stare. Bend down, tie your shoelaces.
        Brown: *if you stare as if at obsidian, your lenses will break*
            down.   Yes.)

—*away, having been, from you, too long*

VI. His Eyes

stare back against me (I the oddity). I feel them,
even from across the room, strip me down
from neck to shoes, until I blink. Green-shirted,
florid in rage at my intrusions, he knows my type:
                              (uppity white
in preppy tweeds and slacks, usual striped tie)—
this outfit I should *not* have worn when I chose
to come to Harlem's station—*costumed* clown
for a place my parents wanted me not to come to.
          No one's taught me how to smile to ease
a stare: I'm pummeled, classed again among heirs
of owners or users. (*My skin can't tell you I'm a Jew,
also segregated, but not in the same way,
as my mother spoke*).

          A man enters now, plump, sweatshirted, sees
us crossed in our own crosshairs, sneers at our contest,
the unnameable fantasies. He glides through our stares
          (briefly shattered)
to find a seat, bald head burnished under hard lights.
          Your eyes drill my leather briefcase, my skin

of learning (Milton, Blake, who pull me back
to foreign shores, far from books about here,
crops of pain your own folk worked.) My reading
you embarrass. What do you read?

Please let me freeze as rabbit, frog;
from grass and stone be indistinct,
*not know so much or learn so fast
how hard it is to be
the only   Negro   in a restaurant
                    only one different*

Or let me have a paper bag to shield my face. May it be brown.
        Not the clothes but my skin chafes me:
the sign of my woundings   verbs inside nouns
        the enslavings erupting   wounds inflicted
        histories of our inflictings   received by muscles beneath
        slackened   then finding sinew and steel to survive

And my own flinch: where?—in this long weep of sorrow
for my birthed and wrongcolor hands entangled with people
I never knew
        even upnorth   indifferent to knowing much
collaborators

History's ghosts: hulks between us standing,
arms crossed to ward off, against
        never surmising an innocence of person,
        or lips that shape a candid ease, or words
        in kind   these centuries
in our skins of ruin, stretched athwart these frames
        unbroken yet.
But your stare bathes my skin:
a gift of balm that gleams to show me pains
your kind did, *do daily live and die through,*
what my kind does against you still.   Repair.
        So John Brown knew, and did what was required;
        so, somewhat, my mother knew and tried to tell.

Beneath our skins there's only skeleton—
that, and blood, that's running or cold:
is there no equity except in death?

When will I imagine a first-time meeting with a Negro,
        anywhere,
that doesn't begin with handshakes rasped like sandpaper?

—*away, having been, from you, too long*

VII. On the Platform

Outside now, peering down the tracks
in fidget: not a long wait, given luck.
I sneak looks at the others: am still the only white.

I wait for the train to take me back
northeast to college. Where is the bright
headlamp of the engine to sheen the tracks?
At thirteen, at 97th Street, standing

and waiting for that thrusting out of force
from the musk of subterranean air,
I wanted, almost, to nudge my mind
north to this station (my wit and feet like snails).
These twenty-odd blocks more I baulked,
and took some five long years to make the walk,

yet I couldn't imagine strolling
calmly through Harlem,
another country, taking time to notice
this and that, or that—hardly
striding down a block in swagger
or dawdling long enough (a tourist
with nothing at stake) to eat a meal.

I have tried to pass
through the color line.
But even above ground
          the very airs seem sorted into shades
and still I have not had,
anywhere, a conversation
with a Negro.

> *—for Shirley Satterfield, who sat-in at the Woolworth's luncheon
> counter (Greensboro, NC, 1960), among the other young women,
> unnamed, along with the Greensboro Four, and for the families of
> Mike Brown, Ramarley Graham and the thousands of others*

WIDER BANDWIDTHS

Between Moons

Close enough, by kayak or skiff,
along hundreds of miles of coast, you see it,
this striped ribbon of life
(just a foot or two high), a cummerbund
girding the sharp-pitched granite
below the Sitka spruce,

streaks of glistering color in layers exposed,
reaping oxygen, sun's warmth,
then lured under surf, and buried twice daily
by tides that lap or buffet, swallow
ground and sky. And then the reverse: tug and withstand.
Moon-bound, predictable.

Invariant, the order of palette:
black shells of barnacles, above the water's brim
a chocolate-blue, then nacre of mussels
as rainbows glimpsed through overcast light, beige-cream limpets,
ivory lichens paling out to white. Fringe
of mosses rimming the array, lemon-green, emerald.

By suction feet, hairs of silk, thread-roots,
each clutches the bedrock of its niche—as eagles, doves,
swallows, choose their swatch of altitude,
count on those densities of air for buoyancy (so crickets,
frogs survive in bandwidths of sound
they've staked out, mastered for eons).

This is the intertidal zone,
where everyone quietly waits
in the sway for the next phase:
washes of air, succor of water, though frigid. And stays put,
in their range of safety. The colonists, chary of risk,
don't poach on a neighbor's stretch of color.

Who wants to dessicate, sunburned too long? Too much
salt is toxic. They gauge their tolerances,
edge slowly upslope, absorbing methane (trained
to endure, given time enough).
The calibrations, coded for balance between drownings
and slack of the tide: may they not shift too fast.
In our zone, I also: between water and sky
bound, planted on soil. At pricks of first air, gasping
for breath under lamplight or sun; now beyond tide's rule,
skinny-dipping under full moons, though hedged
by other surface dwellers here who know they'd choke on
salt,
yet, too far out, test what a snorkel makes viable.

Not smart, risking the murky blues. But we're inclined to push
our colors, allow them to bleed across borders.
Adjacent bands, sworn to protect their water-rights, rise
to defend their crackled sun-bleached farms.
A breathless climb to stake out new terrain ruddies the soils,
mashes the weave of roots beneath.
If air's miasmal, who'll adapt?

Men have stepped on the moon,
outside the swing of tides.
Below, most crisp in heat,

not enough on edge, not

reading ice-melt in time
or well enough. Others

wait impatiently now

for the ritual laving
of the last corpse before

the grey char of us drifts
through air or the body
is sunken down under

Choosing Performances

As she stepped from the limousine
that had brought her from the Cape Town
airport to the hotel, the state-aligned police
made a barricade of bulky arms, interlocked

to keep the mixed and boisterous crowds
from pressing too close to the ballerina,
hailed by some for her limpid arabesques,
spell-binding: from abroad.
                                        But one man,
who later said he had walked from Nyanga,
a black shanty township, many miles distant,
pressed his way forward to speak as she passed
towards the canopied entry.
                                        "I have come
to watch you dance between the rain drops."
She smiled. (The sun that day still shone.)
Though shoved back by police, he smiled in return,
and then, though footsore, accepted
what she spoke next:
                                        "I have come

to this city, in person,
to announce
that I am cancelling
all my performances.
Your great man Nelson
Mandela remains
imprisoned on Robben
Island, on his knees
breaking stone"

(not like that other, the world's legend, who did dance
in Cape Town, traversing the stage *en pointe*,
and later for General Pinochet, and then
for President Marcos, Imelda his wife—
she of the three thousand pair).

Growing Up, Worlds Apart
(August–December 2014)

"What I didn't understand," you replied
as we talked of our first contacts with blacks,
"was their hands, the colors—the browns not wrapped

around to the palms. Where did all that pink
come from—skin like ours?" I nodded, recalled
the plush of tawny cream under the look

of dark leather, in a handclasp. Nothing
rough to trip up kids. But what could have slipped
from our childhood puzzles into the shapes

of dead black bodies, young men unarmed, dropped
to crumple and splay—ten now, this year, killed
by white police (what chance of indictments?).

Tint is what it is. More, what the hand does—
make or wreck; cushion, calm. Who trained our eyes,
stained too white to grasp the tangle of defilements?

The Introductions

A young boy, a teen perhaps,
stands before me as if to speak,
his head bowed towards his shoes.

He has been neatly dressed:
white shirt, buttoned at the collar;
dark trousers, creased.
His skin is almond.

Near his mouth floats
a cloud that blurs his murmurs.

He might flutter off if he could.

About him elders hover; one,
her arm loose under a pale shawl,
ushers him forward, coaxing—
then softly intercedes:

he has heard you are a pianist:
he would like to know
if you will
let you play
some Bach for him.

There is some spasm in the room—
Why would I not play?
—because (it is whispered)
of the color of the skin
of one of you (or both);
he is not sure which.
My face goes ash.

I say: of course,
and ask if I may play
with *him*   later?   His eyes
glow hazel. He nods.

How shall I shade the colors
of my palette?

Afterwards I beckon.
We sit on the piano bench,
hands at rest on our thighs, parallel.

The keys of our instrument
are ebony, ivory. We each,
as we like, may touch.

He sounds out some bare notes,
then a few bars (both hands).

I pick up his pulse and motif.
We invent a duet
(there is no instruction,
save what we are told
by focus of the ears
focus of fingers)

and for maybe three minutes
we improvise   until the phrases
nudge us towards some closure
and so we are just about done

we do be done
and from the keys lift
our hands at the same instant
and then slowly turn,
discover smiles   for what we've done

During this Heavy Snowfall,
Maybe Winter's Last

just now I have been able to picture wings
of monarch butterflies flapping (more splashy

than marbled end-papers in leather-tooled books,
hair-veined, comb-marbled, feathered with peacock eyes,

battling endlessly northwards through air currents
from fir trees near Palomas, in Mexico,

riding their histories of instinct to Hopewell,
right here in Jersey, to the sticky white-sapped

milkweed plants, where they'll spawn larvae by thousands,
and the caterpillars will feed on the leaves,

methodically chomp out huge perforations,
tattered splotches of eye-holes, edges scalloped

like pie-crusts, until they have demolished each
fresh leaf, the spine not exempt, all devoured

to insure their triumph in time as the next
generations may by bookish wisdom wing

its way back to ancestral pines, evading
snows like this one that prods me to imagine

their warm hibernations as if I could
also journey south and then return) and so

I suppose I have begun to remember
a spring still possible, splashed by orange gauds.

Out of Trenton, into the Sourland Mountains, West of Hopewell

Rising from that valley below, a train
beyond my sight of it speeding—some honk
or whistle? But no, this modern engine
holds surprises for me—rightly scaled tones:
from the long first note a perfect third mounts
to the full triad with its dominant.
        Since when does a local railroad's common
locomotive come equipped with its own
hunting horn and fanfare?—more libertine
than the Mozart in Penn Station (that *Eine*
Kleine glop to calm the hordes) but still bound

to spurt just its one sole phrase—unsustained,
sporadic, not shrill enough to frighten
crows: computerized, caught in an engine
running blind through dried fields.
                    An insistent
triad: no *diminuendo*, no loon's
foghorn oboe cries that conjure distant
lakes, wilderness relief for stalled urban
minds, lawn-bound, craving hemlock's scent, and pine's
(beheld after vanishing).
                      Metallic,
these blasts. Still, they hint (back to the tonic)
a tune complete, cleaner than the claxon
of a fire engine's squawk as it grunts,
muscling through snarled-up traffic downtown
(yet London's din was quelled, entranced by Haydn)
and right now! I know why: it's coming soon,
his birthday,
            tomorrow! Beethoven's.
That's why the engine's singing *Beethoven*.
Beethoven's gotten into the engine's
signal, to remind me: he makes it sing

him because he knows I'm in his sonics,
orbiting gleaming through his instruments'
fantasies, though cramped in that steel machine
he's hijacked—past Bonn, or the woods of Vienna
where he strode out to claim, compose his mind.

I am his host: in my skull, Beethoven.
I, his guest, within his fecund garden,
pleroma of triads where inversions
glitter, *millefleurs* sparkle. How he governs,
such a panoply! shimmered from a blind
locomotive, four notes lacking motive—
but the motif he sings: he's got motives
in spades, motivic push to mount octaves,
propulsive, festoons of motifs, dominant
in air, from airwaves unbound and immune.
        Nothing, Ludwig, no one's got your engine,
those tumultuous ears, the inner ones
that shape and stretch my range. Though the train's gone
dead, lost beyond earshot, your mazy designs
inhabit me: you, my drone, now long flown
from that beet-garden origin, Beethoven.
December fifteenth, two thousand seventeen.

The Dash

In pencil, drawn freehand on paper,
a straight line of dashes:
        the bullet,   its trajectory.

The dashes hit the back of
the man running away from
the man with the gun
         twenty feet behind (four inches,
    scaled to the page)—and pass through his chest.

    The dashes then enter the back of
the next man ahead of
the first man shot,   then exit and
    drill through the bulk of
the third man running ahead of
the second man shot.

Eight men are shown shot by the
         single streak of dashes. The
right edge of the page imposes
      a visual limit.

The men are either   eight men shot
    at increasing distances from
    the man with the weapon or
one man shot
      eight times,
      in eight positions
         of flight.

Whether eight men or one man,
   the drawing shows a gun man
        gone wild.
The figures shot are drawn as sticks
with arms, but they are
unarmed.

(The state authorizes men
with regulation-issue firearms
to use lethal force if   they have reason
                                    to believe
their lives are   endangered.)

The figures are also drawn fallen
        dead. Neat horizontal lines
represent their bodies parallel to
                the bottom edge of the page.
The flat lines, with limbs, resemble   stubble.
The drawing is not conceived
                    in perspective.

The viewer supplies the missing
action of the figures, who fall like
        dominos or a
        clock's minute hand dropping swiftly
from noon to three).

The mental effect is that of a frieze
in early photographic studies of motion.
                    The same image
                    is repeated up to
the page's right edge. The onlooker's eye does
        not stop   at the border.

A youngster draws this picture. His dashes
are steady, controlled; the short gaps
between them   standardized also.

        The dashes streak
invisibly home to their target
bodies. No time separates one
shooting from another.
            The times are   always.

By convention, a single missile burns the
     flesh of
     multiple men dashed down
on repeated occasions of
        damage: a hunted population.

The child draws circles
     which stand
     for the heads
     of the shot and felled men.
He fills-them-in with graphite   greyish-
black.   The circle for the man
        with the gun
he leaves white,
     colorless as the paper.

     He draws   our news,
what we've heard,   seen on TV, video:
what his parents   for any past half-year,
may have told or   answered him,
     what he may have
     picked up from friends about the
doom of someone.

No identifying captions are given;
the ones shot could be anyone.

The drawing is thus composite.
Because of the disciplines evident
     (the long dash,
     the piercing of the torso only),
it does not show the fire-bursts of point-blank
     hyphens that struck the chest of
another youngster (the one in   Cleveland,
last December, 2014),
        half an inch distant.

But he knows the drawing is true.
     He cannot pronounce   the
image.

Trench

The inner weep   unheard by each
across the trench   the white sheet chill
stiff as a board   between them wedged
through them as each   turns left or right
to their bed's edge   to clutch so close
embrace the child   the pillows crushed
in foetal curl   for the last time
until night falls   again and each
again cannot   cross the cruel breach
to cry in turn   or unison
or risk a touch   or else caress
to smooth away   the inner weep

for their lost   slain
between them laid
in the white trench
just twelve   their ghost
spawn of their loins
corpse of their care

—for the parents whose children have been murdered

Night-Piece: Firefly

    And I pray
for the intermittent star
in my bedroom lost
this night
    luminescence of firefly
its surging glows or fade-outs
nearly chartreuse
    pray for its escape but not before
this disembodied meteor
gleams again for the sake
of tricking my eyes
guiding them through random
patches of dark
intriguing surprise
appearances
messages
    indecipherable
as it scouts
my body unexpected
in the heat lightly clad
and helps me drift off
warding away the sun-flares
on hubcaps of EMS vehicles
their blue and red flashes in sync
and guards against scenes
of today's or the next day's
blood in waste shed
    and let me pray well enough
for the firefly
whose each pulse flares panic
for a mate but finds
    no moist night grass
and also must intuit
a flight-plan to escape
from extinguishment
before morning light
and the dimming to flatline
prostrate on the hard floor.

Coming to Voice

I

Think how blood thinks its passages
through the body, knows it's pumped to course
through channels familiar, hundreds
of miles—sometimes allowed to reroute

but never free to break restraints
unless the body's damaged (pierced
or shot, clubbed brutishly). It's then
the phrases, sentences ooze out,

the tongue lava-thick, its spitfire
babble more quiet than a child's,
as old-fashioned letters criss-crossed,
illegible. With this fate chanced,

surprised by the smart of live air
smiting fast and so soon (at all),

it speaks aloud through the new mouth
of wound, gash or small gape, an eye

that spies inside, though occluded,
our bodies' common secrecies.

II

What did the bloods of the dying
speak when they were ambushed by trick
at Wounded Knee?—when the Negroes
of East Saint Louis suffered killerwhite
rampage, their black red bloods crying
to glimpse strange sky, or when that man
took at last the assassin's shot

there (the Lorraine Motel), his blood
on that balcony speaking calm
through his doom a decade foreknown,
his tongue now a sheen of his flame,
soon the dark char of his justice.

Who attended each blood's last speech?
Some applauded. Others tarried
to witness the dwindled eddies
of truth spilled against power. Sharp eyes
might from those hidden mouths hear griefs
for clamors hushed, equal weights trashed.

Shed, or cased in veins, the blood's red,
blue blood a fancy of privilege.
Not black blood's gloom, nor the black stain
of miscegenation can dark
the red; rape never tints blood's hue.
Cut any skin (any color),

look. Metaphors that fib too much
blood can't absorb, nor words whose rhymes
make muddles (semen, skin). Only
when blood's revealed to naked air
does it go mute, purpling brown
as it scabs to crust in strange weather.

MARKS OF THE STYLUS

Filaments of Fire

From the core:
fire of magma chilled
then fractured   exposed
at the surface of soil
as rock splotched by lichens,
rough home for cushions
of moss to grasp hold
make crevices   gullies
where rains can gather

for a new-blown seedling
its bare thread of root

push of grass   its first blade
from that matrix reaching
perhaps an inch this year
finally up into air
a periscope to test
the fickle warmths of spring
its winds   and waiting
for the fuller sun
its languid pulse of fire

while we stretch skywards
    heliotropic
cheeks burning or flushed
brainwaves in ascent

as our feet hold down
these igneotropic
bodies   toes and heels
gripping into the crust
the trembling mantle
to tap the earliest heat
harbored and distant
at the planet's core

these our rippling filaments
of flame   more delicate

For Some Box from Tiffany's

If I thought a perfect acorn,
umber, would suffice to adorn

your unjewelled neck, a pendant strung
on no more than a plaited thong

couched in the hollow of your throat
below the apple's bulge, I doubt

I'd seek a more lustrous measure
for your eyes, green as chrysoprase,

that might surpass this primitive
donation of oak nut—retrieved

just now, lying barely aside
my left boot, almost trod under.

Risings

Back then, I guessed, whoever rose to greet
the sun slipped out from wigwam or tipi
to wait for those first throbs of orange blush,
or else (slug-a-bed in felted blankets,

too late for that chill prevenient glow),
rushed out to be blindsided by the orb
already ascended, but still dashed east
to the ledge (late devotions always due):

there to prostrate himself, silently lie
until the sun's hard burn had branded, owned
him, before he dared then turn to behold
those silent rings of power raking the sky.

These days, I edge out from bed, my wife's side,
shuffle past the dog to waddle downstairs;
peep through drawn blinds at low northern skies, check
the temp. By habit, bend; start to unload

the china, knives, detritus from supper,
trying to mute the clatter of plates, clank
of pots (oh, shut up!) at my poor ears still
shuttered by sleep. I strain to remember:

tighten your abs, don't twist the wrong way. Spare
your back, your creaking knees. Still, this privilege:
to own my dishwasher, and these, my own
kitchen basics: my refrigerator,

gas stove—long gone, the hazard-prone hot plate
I bought in college, the type you'll still find
in SROs, homes of the dark—luckless,
wildened at the margins, who reap their heat

straight from a burnishing reddening coil,
electrical pulse, magic snake, no kind
of god to acknowledge—but a spiralled
nautilus, hot, where spitters' spit sizzles.

Down

Each season now, their numbers in free fall,
titmouse, nut-hatch groundward sink, like leaves hushed,
dislodged by a tickling breeze. Featherweight
ounces downed: rot, duff, soil.

At a pond's edge: flecks, shadows as wings lost
past eyesight drift, spied late in sunlight—molt
as leaves blown to shirred ripples, against shore
or dam-grate perched to hush.

Razzmatazz of chain saws:
bite and grind, heartwood gnawed, eaten. Airwaves
nearby shatter, go numb.

How can you expect the birds
to sing when their groves are cut down?
(Thoreau: his sentence, before the clear cuts,
before skies black with passenger pigeons
emptied out, his judgment

on men who sawed by hand, heard the axe-heads
lodge *ch-thuk,* into pith,
yanked the haft loose for the next muscling strokes.)

Toothed blades sing out their burden: elegies
for silence, leaf-homes downed. Who expects speech-
less deafened birds to breed?

What About Speaking?

When each by turns was guide to each,
And Fancy light from Fancy caught . . .
(Tennyson, *In Memoriam, XXIII*)

So I'm expected to know
she *always* leaves the back door
unlatched when she walks the dog?---
and so I am not supposed

to lock the door behind me
if I go out—leaving her,
coming back first, to fumble
for the spare house-key buried

under the brick "*you put* near
that prickly holly," dog-leash
in one hand, maybe also
the terrier's poop in a bag—

afterwards, she tells me this,
after these twenty-six years
and I'm still *doing it wrong.*
(How am I meant to "stand guard"

while she's gone if I don't know
the door's not locked? wasn't told?)
Marriage of our silences!—not
like Tennyson's, telepathic,

when *Thought leapt out to wed with Thought*
Ere Thought could wed itself with Speech—
So embraced, where's argument?
For us, speech unvoiced still asks

consent. How often our dog
will wait while we patch a breach!
Is there some sly god who might
please help us learn to intuit?

Figuring It Out

Still unable, finally, to catch
or keep up, she just baulked right there,
a good distance back on the trail,
stock-still—to coax my turn, hard-put
to say or tell what was the matter—

and stared at me: patient, keen eyes
locked on mine. Did she dream I could see
or do something? I peered straight
back at her, puzzled. I couldn't tell
what the matter might be or was.

Later, maybe a quarter-mile on,
still she was hobbling, dragging
behind. I waited, for we both
needed a water-break. Did she sense
what was the matter? I learned soon,

when I grasped her canteen. My hands
in her fur said: you put her backpack
on wrong. I'd skewed the chest strap: it bound
her right shoulder tight, forced her foreleg
into a limp. That was the matter—

I the dimwit, unable to guess
or suppose that fault. Hadn't she made
beckon with her body?—signaled me,
Backtrack. Please: I can't keep your pace.
Read my personal matters better.

Her tongue slicked my cheek and lips
to say she understood my lapse,
appreciated that at last I'd heard
the matter that her body told
(her troubling crimp I could have forestalled).

Oh, my poor husbandry. Learn how this dog
without bark speaks: see the saying
postures, heaves of lungs—the jobs
that earn the owning. Trees I barely read.
Why should use of tongues matter so much?

On the Rim of the Grand Canyon
of the Yellowstone River, Looking Down

At maybe thirty-odd miles
an hour, how long will it take
these winds to rip from that branch
of the cliff-born lodge-pole pine
the sandwich-baggie whose shreds,
defiant, grasp for bare life?—
oil-slicked and renegade
pennant of our pollutions:
even here, at this chasm cut
by silent booming falls, tatters
of our enterprise.

The Use of Woods

Where did I read of that clinical study done
on vets at the Army's main hospital, Walter Reed?—
showing that if they relaxed with a daily stroll in the woods
nearby, they'd heal just as well as if they'd been

injected on schedule, made calm by cocktails
of new drugs, now cleared through their last strict trials
(cost-free, those woods, even for troops transported out
from daily combat-work where they'd lost

a limb, their minds, or half their bloodied unit).
How those shadowy murmurs of leaves, the eyes' reach
for bedded moss, whiffs of spearmint tingling those maims
of stress or blasted parts, hint reprieve from firefight haunts,
          though never release.

No matter. I too need such a venturing back
to some dense woods where I might have lost her,
a terrain in common?--go to ground, pick up, with luck,
her scent or spot the quickened phantom of her ghost,

then for our solace coax her back (my ten-year's Queen
of Heaven: that dog off-lead, paws to her ears obedient—
(comparing great things with small, of course, but not
knowing, these days, the difference. Even
these weeks, since her tumor invaded, then shattered
          her brain like shrapnel.)

Bone

Scapula, rib; femur, joint—in a field,
on trail: whoever spots a scattering
of bones will piece out, guess a death-scene wild
but staged enough to visualize a plot

that makes of any sudden bloodying
at the throat a destiny. Shrieks are mute
if the dying's welcomed or quick; the pain
of crumpling down may ease the wracking strain

of being common quarry; deep, the bite
of hunger's satisfaction—what bargains,
struck for them long before they met! And then
with a wince, the witness blinks out the sight,

"composes the place" prior to furor:
now the prey grazes, sidles unaware
of being stalked—its viscera, burden
of innards still trussed by ribcage, backbone,

legs well planted on terrain that's secure
(spliced from TV, scenes in museums). Who hefts
a bone may ask how such a thing conjoins
in space a spot of time—and yet harder,

must guess (as I, no deft anatomist)
what part of me (who trotted once) this piece
calls kin? Knobbed unsyllabled shape, creviced
with a pulley's groove, graceful as a spool

or muscle-hinge—but how can you scale

a beast whose measurements a sole bone thwarts.
A joint?—what length of bone did it socket,
sinews anchor? I probe some flesh of me

to find a correspondent place—elbow?—
wrestle our bodies' histories, touch fresh clues.
Death's candid token, but no *memento
mori* now; here, mid-day, my analogue

and leveler. We're all just passing through,
need water, a cave or pelts, some forage-
turf to share with others when fodder's sparse,
and a knack for nimbling through disasters

shrewdly. Dry bone in my palm: not hard stone,
nor marrow-rich and quick. Are there others,
fractured, baked, that itch for some reunion?—
as Atlas, splayed through rock, in his mountains

dreams still to be pliant. My fingers rub
this bone against my cheek—grain like pumice,
a sandpaper, these roughed-up caresses
that hoard the sun's chilled pulse to give surprise—

and let it fall to the ground, on leaf-duff,
grass. How long will it take before someone
names its right name? In this small clearing strewn,
what's sculpture of nature but bone detached?

Dining Together

—for P. L.

Remember when we tried not to stare
at couples like those over there, the ones
eating without visible thoughts of talking
to each other?—twosomes, no matter where
(Augusto's, The Half-Moon), scarcely looking
up to meet each other's eyes or murmur
their preference for some cheese or sweet dessert.

Had they been becoming old together,
coupled so long, each one's first love? (we mused)—
they knew the fissures of the other's brain,
might even claim to hear their munches, see
each bite of cuttlefish or haddock wind
down the other's package of bowels, even
chant the rhythms, churns of rumination.

So much more love between them learned by now—
the many treaties ironed out, smooth-pressed
as these napkins, linen, white! But we guessed:
there must lurk (under the table, between
chair-legs, flesh-legs) their feuding stifled imps,
and dancing through our dazzling pheromones,
gilt as silverware, quipped, "Become *them*? Never!"

But have. Like those we watched before, silent
when we venture out (while knowing more
of us than we of them). Seated catty-corner
though out of touch with touch, we still surmise
our much-unruffled love. See these dozen
little-necks outspread!—while we, unshucked, rue
the smoulder of embers in ancient groins.

Even so, does your brow wrinkle, ask if
a pun, or riddle or some lesser twist
might not be welcomed to breach the buffers
of these quietudes, austere and Trappist?—
such a spice to stir these moods as we wait,

this frost-bit dusk, for something appetent
to tide us through endurance to the end,
whichever one's comes first.

Girl in the Rain, on a Tree-Lined Street (Princeton, New Jersey)

There she is, in her very pink Wellies,
this day of dark downpour, towards me
chirping, "Good morning!"— some glee released
in her, secret as a flock of butterflies,
to share with this most surprised and closely-
hooded stranger in his drab rain-jacket.

      "Good Day to you too," I warble back:
      "have a great day at school!"— and she
            (in our antiphony):

"You too!"—and with her umbrella three times pokes
the drenching sky (her salutes to me, who tote
                    no backpack)

and then strides on, but soon twirls back, having noted
that I must be two feet taller than she, and my hood
hiding hairs maybe as grey as her grandad's
or even her father's, and pipes out: "Well, have a great day,
                    no matter what!"

I grin, "Oh, yes—I too will write and read"—
and amble on, mulling my day's curriculum.

In the Museum: On Viewing
an Oversized Photograph

of a child, prepubescent,
wearing a green-and-white
polka dot skirt

"nude above the waist"
the curator (or curatrix) attests
on a plaque affixed at the right

not (as one might think)   naked
shirtless   blouse-less   topless   bare

and tell me when
or if   a boy or girl becomes flat-
chested

no matter what the name assigned
to bluish-grey of lake or pond behind

The Fit: An Epistle

—for C. S.

"Dear C—" (so another poet also wrote),
     When they sent me a Size 36B in black
(preshaped fiberfill, bare of any lace),
instead of the Mens Swimwear (click, scroll down),
Speedo (click) in red (click), that I'd ordered
to flatter my vanities, I wondered:
did the Macy's people know something
about my afterlife that I should ponder?

I tried it on, of course, my most recent
life-long partner also wanting a gander,
though admitting a preference for me as is.
Not a fit. But some omen, still, or hint?

There had been, of course, *Pinafore, Patience*
and other operettas, when my school-friends
and I (such young soprano, alto voices
still uncracked) were cross-dressed by our mothers—
flounced-up as damsels, maidens or fairies
to sing the roles they never had (or be
the daughters they never had but wanted)—
so they hooked us into their still-silky brassieres
and filled them (o! the giggles) with their husbands'
tennis balls (too firm or stacked for some)
or else a padding more demure.

That time, too, a bad fit,
               but portent
of what, last year at Kajuraho, make me gawk:
the perfect breasts of those Hindu temples' dancers
in mythic copulations with their gods
(Vishnu, Shiva), their huge naked sandstone orbs
impressing the sky with such a ritual bulge
that not half a continent away Pythagoras throbbed,
swaying in rhythm with those voluminous globes,

the dancers' pulse in heat, and theorized
by number the music of the spheres.

But for me? Thanks to that stock-boy or -girl
who made a mindless swipe at the passing shelves,
I had a chance to try on, flirt with my own
     hermaphrodite: for an intergalactic second
become complete, glimpse myself kin to that Venus
of Velazquez who holds her mirror down
to view, between her thighs, on canvas,
whatever there her organs are): be androgyne—
and pose the cosmic clasp of opposites,
jump-start my pending metamorphosis
to woman, if not nightingale or ox.
How, for the shapes of my lives to come, might
I know which many sins of mine are venial,
and how for punishings shall I be cast?

No matter. This carnal, daily balding male
bores me now. The dangling bra's a relief
for this short while remaining to my end-game—
beyond the boundaries of this old torso
(stiff, a rectangle box): my habits fit,
my choices made unfit by choices
     chromosomal, not mine.
                       It's not the lure
of frilly lace I miss but—? the swimming
as a mermaid, cavorting with other
damsels, topless, in the seas (and careless
for whatever parts the silver scales conceal
without a Speedo!) Not needing to ask
my brain permission to transgress, splash,
cavort a while transfigured in the waves.
     That Macy's goof enticed me to wonder
about the other swerves. Did you surmise,
dear C— (keenly pitched, and knowing me then)
how gingerly I sought to keep wrapped up
those "other" gestures most guys have been trained

against: hand on the hip ("your" way, not "mine"),
the no-no pinkie twiddling air from glass
or teacup, stereotyping falsetto.

Could I have trusted you with my splinter
of truth (you, "sinister," patterned leftwards
but still straight, chaste and honest in your tongue)—
while I, raised to be powered by the codes
of the dexterous male, strove against my genes'
inheritance? Might we have shared our turns
of flesh? Or is it only now, when age
gives me flex for what's eccentric (beyond
prescription's bounds) that I permit me (yes!)
such fantasies?
             But were you too ever
inquisitive about your other side?—
Nel mezzo del cammin, our other kinds
of middle ways, straddling the roadway's crown
(swaying a little bit to left or right but not
off balance nor wrongly tilted at hip or joint,
though sometimes wishing to stray a little bit more).

Portrait of Speech

So as I come through his door, I'm holding
my boot in one hand, and waving its tongue
in the other. Luigi, I say, I've lost my tongue.
He grins, "You talk too much" (punning

already) and adds: my tongue is crackled.
Overuse, I reply (he knows I write
and teach). He can fix the loose tongue, sew it
back to the boot's mouth, or?—make a fresh tongue,

brand new. I shake my head. I don't speak "fresh"
any more. His eyebrows rise. He beckons,
"*Sedersi, prego.*" I catch his gesture
(sit), but stand. When he turns to his workbench,

wagging my tongue behind him like his tail,
I spy the gear of his strange trade—cutters,
steel jack (foot-shaped), pliers, trimmers, glue pots,
foot-wear of strangers (in my way). He squats,

shoulders and back rounded. Uccello might
have painted him. I hear sounds of his work
at the stitcher machine. "Maybe you'd like
a new inner sole?" he calls (silly joke).

Do I look so worn out?" He twists, then winks.
"And no new heel," I add. But *does* the boot
need more repairs?—am I foolish to say
no to advice, whatever cost? I tout

his craft. "Luigi, You're the best. I wouldn't
ask anyone else to repair my shoes." "*Grazie,*
Signor Harris." He comes back with my boot
aloft in the air between us: his trophy.

He tugs the tongue. "Double-stitched to the mouth

of the upper. Better than new. Oil it.
(not too much). Who likes a slick tongue? Neatsfoot
is good. You'll never lose this tongue again."

Oh. "And it won't ever fork?" No more flex,
wiggle or wag? I'm pleased. "See these eye holes?"
he pinches one—"*forte*, strong. The laces:
to keep your tongue tied while rambling." He smiles,

hands me the boot, restored, and doesn't ask
enough (five dollars). But as I'm leaving,
I'm struck: it's the day before New Year's Eve
Day, so I say, "Luigi, *come se dice*,

Happy New Year in *Italiano*?"
He says by habit, flatly, *Buon' Anno*.
Seeing my face cloud (nothing more festive,
florid?), he offers *Felice Anno*

Nuovo!—ah! sparkling, upbeat! I speak it back
to him ("*Grazie*"), then fervently add,
"Have a Healthy New Year." His brow's furrowed.
Healthy?—his eyes squinch. How can he make puns

and not know "healthy"? Perhaps a cognate,
bella fortuna?—but money's not what
I mean (though it might help as plastic shoes
eat market share). So I shift tongues, try out

my little French: "*À votre santé.*" "*Non
e permesso; pas de français.*" He scowls
at the French. OK, but does he *get* it?
Parts of a language we've got in common,

but not the right one. He opens his palms,
asking help. Stalled, all I can do is shout:
HAVE HEALTHY *Buon' Anno!*—again *niente*.

Dumb: no reason why brute lung power should mean

a meaning to anyone. But then
he risks a possible phrase, finds sunshine;
he beams. "Ah, *come il vino . . . salute!*"
He raises his right hand. "*Buona Salute.*"

Salute, right, like Spanish, *salud*. I toast
him, "*Buona Salute, Luigi*"—and then
I salute him, since he's come to the States
post-war, not long since, and I (a writer)

should know my Dante, Petrarch, Primo Levi—
my genes snarled in Europe's roots. Luigi bows
a small bow, "*Grazie.*" "No, *grazie* to you—
you've improved all my tongues. Now I won't need

to break in new hiking boots." Luigi smiles.
A break in his cobbling, this visit?—the chat,
speaking in tongues, ours, as we are able,
throating the words we find available.

Night-Piece: The Well

And I pray
for the guardian of the guard
concealed further off
attentive each night
for whatever thuds louder
than heartbeat or pulse
the scratches of stones
that they not be
picked off or garroted
no matter their armoring
and that the waters not
those any nights   be poisoned
diverted (with all our unknown
dawns to come)
and pray that the guardians
survive for the sake
of their pumping lungs
whose breaths must yield us
names for markers we need
to trace some shadow of path
or for the other sake
of some map that must
survive for others
needing   guidance
to that well at night
though some will be barred
their satisfaction's need
or not make it back

Ghost of a Poem

There is some clutter of words that squats
here, blocking what I almost glimpsed to write.
      Boulders of Inca, Mycenae
thwart my glance along paths of my eyes,

stubbing my sockets, scraping ridges
into my pale cheeks.
      To the beat
of hammers pounded through airborne frets,
the slaves chisel marks of their lords,

my winced spyholes. For monuments
ordered by Cheops, royal Khufu,
they sand, sand to a sheen, polish limestone
slab facings that lure the sun's kiss, hide tufa.

Each slab glares misuse of heart or hand—
not mummied (chambered as Cheops) but lugged
to off-site troughs for anonymous dead.
      Baked by sun, tawny or black their skins,

they've left no profile on a wall,
much less a lifted arm
               to gesture me
a few first steps beyond this boulder
towards the glimpse of blur I thought I might recall.

When

Since time is running out for me
to say about
> the currents of oceans
> gulls on their errands
> above wind-lashed palms

And time is running out for me
to say about
> the horses, their riders
> and the cattle, the beasts
> of burden, oxen yoked
> to plow the many fields

And time is running out for me
to say about
> the   other chattel
> bodies caught and shackled
> transshipped and bought
> enslaved for free profit

While time runs short for me
to say about
> women abused to breed
> for the owners who used them
> the children, men schooled by whip

Time's run out for me
to cough up phlegm and tell
> of whites who told
> in schools the whitest lies
> that could be told
> about   our liberties
> (and *boy! was I sold!*)

So time keeps running back to me
stands still at my front door
> harries me to speak
> though I at the sill
> poise to falter